Eminem

by Z.B. Hill

Superstars of Hip-Hop

Alicia Keys

Beyoncé

Black Eyed Peas

Ciara

Dr. Dre

Drake

Eminem

50 Cent

Flo Rida

Hip Hop:
A Short History

Jay-Z

Kanye West

Lil Wayne

LL Cool J

Ludacris

Mary J. Blige

Notorious B.I.G.

Rihanna

Sean "Diddy" Combs

Snoop Dogg

T.I.

T-Pain

Timbaland

Tupac

Usher

Eminem

by Z.B. Hill

Mason Crest

Eminem

Mason Crest
370 Reed Road
Broomall, Pennsylvania 19008
www.masoncrest.com

Printed and bound in the United States of America.

First printing
9 8 7 6 5 4 3 2 1

          Library of Congress Cataloging-in-Publication Data

Hill, Z. B.
  Eminem / by Z.B. Hill.
     p. cm. − (Superstars of hip hop)
  Includes index.
  ISBN 978-1-4222-2518-9 (hardcover) − ISBN 978-1-4222-2508-0 (series hardcover) − ISBN 978-1-4222-2544-8 (softcover) − ISBN 978-1-4222-9220-4 (ebook)
 1. Eminem (Musician)−Juvenile literature. 2. Rap musicians−United States−Biography−Juvenile literature. I. Title.
  ML3930.E46H55 2012
  782.421649092−dc22
  [B]
                    2011005800

Produced by Harding House Publishing Services, Inc.
www.hardinghousepages.com
Interior Design by MK Bassett-Harvey.
Cover design by Torque Advertising & Design.

Publisher's notes:
• All quotations in this book come from original sources and contain the spelling and grammatical inconsistencies of the original text.
• The Web sites mentioned in this book were active at the time of publication. The publisher is not responsible for Web sites that have changed their addresses or discontinued operation since the date of publication. The publisher will review and update the Web site addresses each time the book is reprinted.

DISCLAIMER: The following story has been thoroughly researched, and to the best of our knowledge, represents a true story. While every possible effort has been made to ensure accuracy, the publisher will not assume liability for damages caused by inaccuracies in the data, and makes no warranty on the accuracy of the information contained herein. This story has not been authorized nor endorsed by Eminem.

Contents

Hip-Hop lingo

A **record** is a group of songs played on a plastic disc by a phonograph. Today, a lot of people still call CDs and MP3s "records."

A **prescription** is a drug that has to be given to you by a doctor.

If someone is **abusing** something, it means he's taking too much of something, or using it incorrectly.

ADHD is a condition that makes it hard for a person to focus on one thing for a long time.

Rap is a kind of music where rhymes are chanted, often with music in the background. When people rap, they make up these rhymes, sometimes off the top of their heads.

Talent shows are contests where people compete to show how good they are at something.

A **recording studio** is a place where musicians go to record their music and turn it into CDs.

Rhyming is a musical way of putting similar-sounding words together.

A **producer** is the person in charge of putting together songs. A producer makes the big decisions about the music.

An **album** is a bunch of songs made to go together on a CD.

Chapter 1

Struggle to Survive

The year is 2003. The movie is called *8 Mile*. It is based on the life of rapper Eminem. He is already a hip-hop star, and soon he will be a movie star too. One of the songs Eminem has written for his movie is called "Lose Yourself." The words of the song are Eminem's advice to himself. They talk about taking the chances you have. They talk about losing yourself in music.

In 2003, Eminem had made it big. On the outside, he seemed to have everything. Millions of **record** sales had made him rich and famous. But on the inside, he was still very much a normal guy. In fact, even as a millionaire, he had new problems to deal with. He had come so far, but he still had a long way to go.

Marshall Mathers

Eminem was born Marshall Bruce Mathers III on October 17, 1972. He was born in St. Joseph, Missouri. His mom, Debbie, was only 17 when he was born. She had married Marshall's dad, Marshall Bruce Mathers II, when she was just 15.

The family moved to North Dakota when Marshall was still a baby. Marshall's dad took a job at a hotel. But Debbie and Marshall's dad fought a lot. Debbie didn't like her husband's mood swings. She took her son back to Missouri. In 1975, Marshall's parents divorced.

The next few years were hard ones for Debbie. She worked at a lot of different jobs. She left Marshall with his father's aunt and uncle. They took good care of him. In many ways, this was

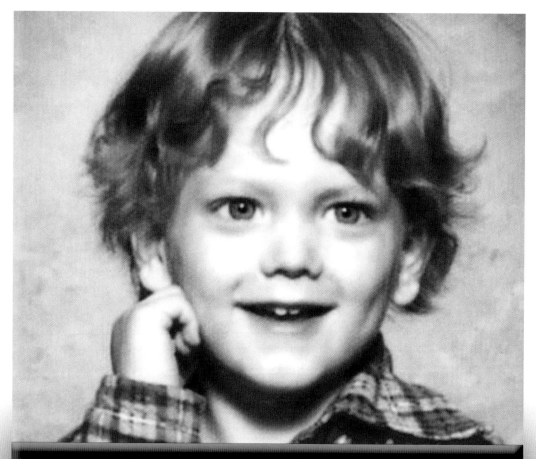

As a small boy, Marshall never had a stable home life for any extended period of time. His parents were divorced when he was very young, and after his mother left Missouri and moved to Detroit, his life changed forever.

the only stable home he had as a child. It wouldn't last for long, though. When he was still young, his mom took him and moved to Detroit, Michigan. Detroit would change his life forever.

Living on the Edge

Debbie and Marshall were almost always poor. They could not afford to live in nice neighborhoods. So they lived in run-down houses and trailer parks instead. Eminem said later, "We kept getting kicked out of every house we were in. I believe six months was the longest we ever lived in a house." On top of that, Marshall was usually almost the only white kid in all-black neighborhoods. He had to quickly learn how to blend in. Or else risk getting beat up.

The family moved so much that Marshall went to at least 20 different schools. It was hard for a kid. As soon as he got used to one place, they moved to another. He couldn't make friends. And always being the "new kid" made him a target for bullies. He told *Rolling Stone* magazine, "Kids are mean to other kids. School is a tough thing to go through."

Trouble at Home

Things were not much better at home. Eminem says that Debbie was **abusing prescription** drugs. He also said that Debbie told him he had **ADHD**. He said she did this so that she could get a drug for ADHD called Ritalin.

Debbie had many boyfriends. She was with one man, named Fred Samra Jr., for five years. Debbie and Fred had a son together, named Nathan. Marshall later called Fred "the closest thing I had to a father figure." He also felt close to his half-brother Nathan. But Debbie had trouble caring for Nathan. The courts sent Nathan to a foster home. Eminem would later ask Nathan to come live with him. But at the time, it was a sad good-bye for the half-brothers.

Good-Bye, High School

By his teen years, Marshall was living just outside of Detroit. He lived in a rough neighborhood across from 8 Mile Road. Most of the time, he stayed with his grandma. But he sometimes visited his mom and half-brother at the nearby trailer park.

When Marshall turned 14, he started at Lincoln High School. He didn't last very long. He was smart, but he didn't like school. He said later, "I failed ninth grade three times, but I don't think it was necessarily because I was stupid. I didn't go to school. I couldn't deal." When he was 17, Marshall dropped out of school for good. He began working as a cook and dishwasher. He made only $5.50 an hour.

Marshall Becomes Eminem

School hadn't worked out for Marshall. But it did change his life. At school, he had fallen in love with a type of music called **rap**. One day, his uncle Ronnie played the rap song "Reckless" by Ice-T. Marshall knew he had found something special. After that, he jumped right into the local hip-hop scene in high school. He joined a group called Soul Intent. He rapped at **talent shows** in the neighborhood.

Marshall began to work very hard at rap. For the first time in his life, he wanted to be good at something. So he started to hang out with a friend named Mike Ruby. Mike had a **recording studio** in his basement. The boys put their songs on tapes. They practiced their **rhyming** skills. Marshall began to work on "the inside rhyme." An inside rhyme puts many words that rhyme into the same line. It was also during this time that Marshall came up with his rap name, M&M. The first "M" was for Marshall, the second for Mathers.

But Marshall had trouble finding people to listen to his music. The hip-hop scene in Detroit was mostly black. No one wanted to listen to a white boy rap. But Marshall didn't want to give up. He became a "battle MC." A battle MC goes back and forth with other MCs on stage. They make fun of each other, insult each other, and try to be the best rapper. Marshall often battled at a Detroit music store called the Hip Hop Shop.

Eminem's troubled relationship with his mother Debbie was depicted in the movie *8 Mile*. In the film, actress Kim Basinger played Marshall's mother. Debbie Mathers has sued her son for his negative depictions of her in his music.

Then his big break came. A local **producer** named Marky Bass heard Marshall rapping. He invited the young man to his studio. Bass later said, "I dropped everything I was doing and I put everything I had into this kid." Bass knew Marshall had something

This photo of Marshall Mathers and Kimberly Ann Scott was taken in the 1990s, before Marshall became famous. His on-again, off-again relationship with Kim would make headlines as they went through a cycle of marriages and divorces.

special. In 1996, he helped him make an **album** called *Infinite*. By then, Marshall had changed his name from M&M to Eminem.

But it wasn't going to be that easy. *Infinite* only sold a few hundred copies. It looked like his career was over before it even started.

Eminem and Kim

When Eminem was 15, he had met a 13-year-old girl named Kimberly Ann Scott. She was a lot like him. She came from a troubled home too. She had grown up in the same Detroit neighborhoods. The two hit it off and started dating.

There was something special about this relationship. They were together a long time. Then, in 1995, Kim became pregnant. Knowing he was about to be a father made Eminem work that much harder. He wanted to give his daughter the things he'd never had. And he knew that $5.50 an hour wasn't going to cut it.

His daughter, Hailie Jade Scott, was born on December 25, 1995. Eminem later said that this was the best day of his life. But the joy didn't last. *Infinite* didn't sell, and Kim and Eminem broke up. When Kim wouldn't let him see his newborn daughter, it was too much. The rapper tried to kill himself.

Eminem didn't die, though. Instead, he got a second chance. Eminem had a change of heart. He decided he would make a new start. He would begin rapping again. He would be a father to Hailie, no matter what. Things were about to change in a big way.

Hip-Hop lingo

Lyrics are the words in a song.

A **demo** is a rough, early version of a CD before the real thing comes out.

An album goes **platinum** when it sells more than 1,000,000 copies.

A **controversy** is created when someone does something that causes a lot of people to argue or get upset.

Chapter 2

Slim Shady Is Born

The mid-1990s were not easy for Eminem. He got back together with Kim. That made him happy. But now he had a girlfriend and a daughter to care for. He was broke. His album hadn't sold. For a while, he gave up music. He worked 60-hour weeks and made very little money. Kim and Eminem had to move into Eminem's mom's house. It was not a happy time.

A New Voice

Eminem couldn't give up his dream of being a musician. But he needed to try something new. He saw that many rappers used an "alter ego" to make their music. An alter ego is a character created to say things a person can't say himself. One day, Eminem knew who his alter ego would be: Slim Shady.

Shady was a bad guy. He dealt drugs, killed people, and did other horrible things. Eminem was tough and could say some harsh things. But Slim Shady took it to a whole new level. Eminem let Slim Shady

Eminem's innovative sound and complex rhyming eventually won him an MTV award in 1999. Describing himself as neither East Coast nor West Coast, but influenced by both, Eminem's unique style was a big hit with audiences everywhere.

take over his raps. He explored the dark side of his own life. Slim rapped about being poor. He rapped about dead-end jobs, drugs, and not having a place to sleep. These new **lyrics** were fierce.

Producer Marky Bass was excited about Eminem's new sound. In 1997, he brought him back to the studio to record a **demo**. They called it *The Slim Shady EP*. Using his Slim Shady character, Eminem rapped about lots of dark stuff. And people liked it. In fact, people started to finally pay attention to Eminem's music.

Eminem's drive to make it in the music world fueled his album *The Slim Shady EP*, recorded with the help of Marky Bass. Here, Eminem performs before a live audience at a small show in Michigan during 1997, wearing a Slim Shady t-shirt.

Welcome to the Big Time

Eminem's demo ended up in the hands of a big shot named Jimmy Iovine. He was the head of one of rap's biggest labels, Interscope Records. Iovine passed the demo to Dr. Dre, who also liked what he heard. He decided to help Eminem make it even better. Together, they produced *The Slim Shady LP*.

The two made a good team. *The Slim Shady LP* came out in 1999 and went triple **platinum**. The song "My Name Is" became a huge

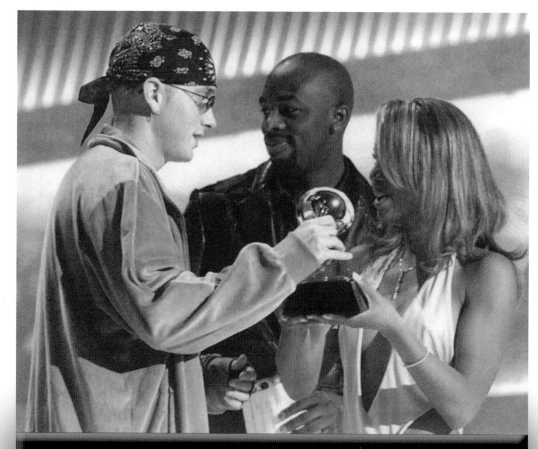

Rapper Eminem accepts his award for Best Rap Album at the 43rd Grammy Awards. He has won nine Grammy awards over the course of his career, including three in the category of Best Rap Album.

Influential rapper and producer Dr. Dre performs with Eminem at the opening of the Experience Music Project in Seattle, Washington. The project is an interactive museum of music designed to teach people about the creative process in American music.

hit single. Everything seemed to happen at once. Eminem became a millionaire overnight. He won a Grammy for Best Rap Album in 2000. And to top it all, he and Kim finally got married!

Controversy

There was no doubt about it. Eminem had become a hip-hop star. But the new album also brought a lot of **controversy**. Slim Shady talked about doing violent acts against women. He even rapped about murdering his wife!

This upset a lot of people. Eminem had to explain that he wasn't Slim Shady. In fact, Slim Shady wasn't real. He was a character made up to tell stories. Eminem said he was just doing what authors do in books—making up a character that does bad things. He

Demonstrators from the gay rights group GLAAD rally outside the 2001 Grammy Awards to protest Eminem's nomination. They felt that his use of offensive language and the hateful attitude expressed toward gays in his songs should not be rewarded.

also felt like Slim Shady was funny. He wanted people to see that the horrible things had another side to them. At first they made you wince or shudder. But when he told them in a funny way, sometimes it made the painful stuff easier to handle.

The Marshall Mathers LP

But not many people saw it that way. The controversy continued. But Eminem didn't let it slow him down. In 2000, he made *The Marshall Mathers LP.* This album became even more popular than *The Slim Shady LP!*

By now, Eminem had a lot of fans. His music was good, but his lyrics were what people really liked. At the time, most hip-hop music was about sex and getting lots of money. Eminem's lyrics were different. He chose to rap about personal stuff, like his struggles to be a good dad. Or how he wanted to love his mom more. Or how he was a bad husband sometimes. His raps might be rude, but at least they were honest.

Fans listened because they related to the lyrics. Many had rough childhoods, bad relationships with parents, and were angry at the world. Just like Eminem.

He had begun to see his dream become a reality. He had reached the top of the hip-hop world. He finally had money to take care of the people he loved. But his personal life was about to take a dangerous turn.

Hip-Hop lingo

When someone's on **probation**, he is allowed out of prison as long as he obeys certain rules—such as not doing drugs.

Chapter 3

The Troubles in Eminem's World

Eminem had written some harsh things about people in his life. Both his mom and his wife took some hard hits in his songs. In many of his lyrics, Eminem rapped about his mom's drug abuse. She didn't like this at all. She filed a lawsuit against her son. She claimed he had ruined her character. She wanted him to pay her 10 million dollars.

Sticking with his usual style, Eminem rapped about this in a song called "Marshall Mathers." In it, Eminem said he started abusing drugs because of his mom. This just made his mom madder.

Things got still worse between Eminem and his family. His mom, his aunt, and his uncle all wanted money from him. They claimed he had promised them money when he got rich, but that he had not followed through and paid up. Eminem finally agreed to pay his mother a small amount of money to end the fighting.

Troubles with Kim

For a while, home life was happy for Eminem. He lived with his wife Kim and his daughter Hailie. They also took care of Kim's niece,

Alaina. Eminem loved having two little girls around the house. But Kim and Eminem still had serious problems to work out.

In 2000, only one year after Kim and Eminem married, Eminem got in a fight and was arrested. He had to pay a fine of $100,000 dollars. He was also put on **probation** for two years. The whole thing was enough to make Kim very upset. Eminem filed for divorce a few months later.

Eminem expresses his regrets about the incident with John Guerra to reporters in a courtroom in April 2001. He was placed on two years' probation. The probation had positive aspects, as it forced the rapper to end his drug use.

Father Figure

This time it was Kim who was arrested. She was put in jail for doing drugs. So Hailie and Kim's niece, Alaina, lived full-time with Eminem. He took his role as a dad very seriously. Eminem wanted to give them the father he had never had. He told *Rolling Stone* his goals as a parent are simple: "Teach them right from wrong as best I can, try not to lose my temper, try to set guidelines and rules and boundaries. Never lay a hand on them. Let them know it's not right for a man to ever lay his hands on a female. Despite what people may think of me and what I say in my songs . . . I'm tryin' to teach them and make them learn from my mistakes I'm not sayin' I'm the perfect father, but the most important thing is to be there for my kids and raise them the right way."

Eminem's fatherly duties didn't stop there. He also took over caring for his younger half-brother, Nathan. He had always wanted to help Nathan. He saw the same bad stuff that happened in his childhood happening in Nathan's. So he took the young man under his wing.

Probation did a lot of good for Eminem. It kept him off drugs and out of trouble. It also helped him control his temper. As 2002 arrived, he was putting his life back together. And this time, his plans went beyond just music.

Hip-Hop lingo

An **alcoholic** is someone who is addicted to beer, wine, or liquor.
Elections are how the United States and many nations choose people to
be in charge of the country.
Music is **political** when it talks about the government or about social
problems.
A **tour** means to travel around and play music for people at concerts.
Rehab is a place where people who have addictions can go to get better.
Someone who is **addicted** to something cannot stop using or doing that
thing, even though he may want to.

Chapter 4

New Horizons

In 2002, Eminem made his next album, called *The Eminem Show*. Once again, it was filled with harsh lyrics. It insulted the "boy bands" of the time, like NSYNC. It took aim at other musicians, too, such as Limp Bizkit and Moby. But overall it was less violent than his earlier albums. *The Eminem Show* was about personal problems. It focused more on his daughters and his relationship with Kim.

The Big Screen

Most of the attention that year went to Eminem's first movie. It was called *8 Mile*, and it was a huge success. It was based on Eminem's own life, but it wasn't his exact story. His character's name is Jimmy "Rabbit" Smith Jr. He is a poor high school dropout who lives with an **alcoholic** mother. Like Eminem, Jimmy is a white boy who dreams of becoming a rapper.

8 Mile was a serious movie. It wasn't just a way for Eminem to sell his music. Eminem wanted to be sure the movie didn't seem phony. He wanted every detail to be perfect. He wanted the movie to seem true to life.

The movie's director was Curtis Hanson. He wanted to do the movie because he saw hip-hop as important to young people. He said, "No one's helping kids figure out where they're going—not just in the inner cities but in the suburbs. Hip-hop comes out of that. It is a voice for people who don't have another voice."

Eminem agreed. He had his own reasons for doing the movie, though. He wanted to show how rap helped him survive his childhood. Rap was everything to him. "This was my whole life. If I lost a battle at the hip-hop shop when I was coming up, it literally tore me apart inside," he said.

Director Curtis Hanson speaks with Eminem on the set of *8 Mile*. Hanson, who had previously directed such films as *L.A. Confidential* and *The Hand That Rocks the Cradle*, felt *8 Mile* would give him the chance to explore a hidden portion of society.

Eminem performs at the MTV Europe Music Awards in Rome. With him onstage were 68 children under the age of 10, brought for his performance of "Just Lose It," a parody of Michael Jackson that references his child molestation cases.

8 Mile was a huge success. People connected with the story about surviving the rough streets of Detroit. Eminem even won an Academy Award for the song "Lose Yourself," which he made for the movie.

More Controversy

Eminem's next album, *Encore*, created more controversy. One of its songs, "Just Lose It," insulted the pop star Michael Jackson. Jackson was very well loved in the hip-hop community. Many people who had stood by Eminem in the past decided they could no longer support him.

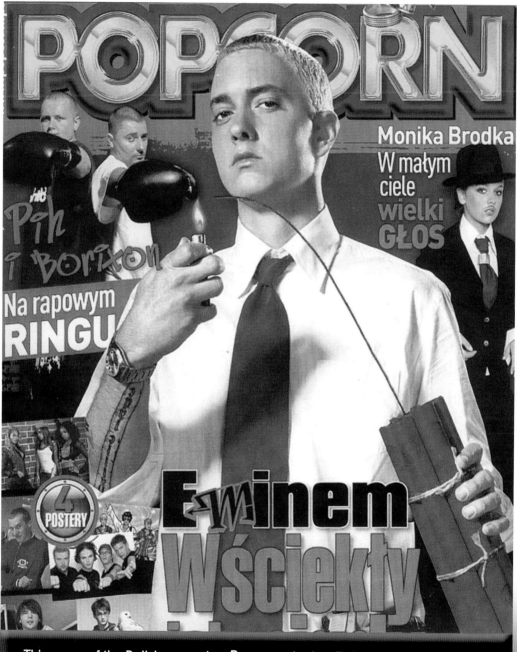

This cover of the Polish magazine *Popcorn* depicts Eminem lighting a stick of dynamite, perhaps a reference to the fire-storms his music usually incites. In 2004 he was criticized for his parody of Michael Jackson, which many people in the entertainment industry did not appreciate.

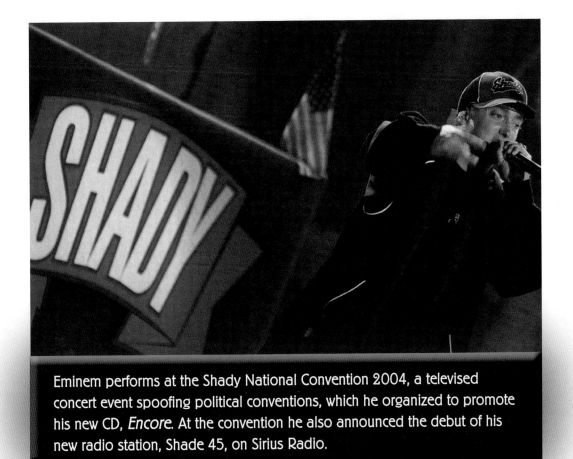

Eminem performs at the Shady National Convention 2004, a televised concert event spoofing political conventions, which he organized to promote his new CD, *Encore*. At the convention he also announced the debut of his new radio station, Shade 45, on Sirius Radio.

Encore did not sell as well as his other albums. But Eminem had his sights set on bigger things.

Speaking Up

There was a lot going on in the United States in 2004. The country was about to choose a new president. The Iraq War had been going on for over a year. Eminem was not happy with the way things were going. So a week before the **elections** he made a song called "Mosh." It spoke out strongly against president George W. Bush. The song asked people to vote against Bush. It was Eminem's first **political** song.

A Tour Ends Early

In 2005, Eminem began his first **tour** in three years. The **tour** started off in the United States and did great. But when it came time to go to Europe, Eminem canceled. He shocked his fans when he said he'd be going to **rehab** instead.

Eminem had struggled with drugs in the past. But this time he was **addicted** to a legal drug—sleeping pills. Eminem knew legal drugs could be just as dangerous, though. His experience with his mother had taught him that. So he made the right move and quickly got help.

In 2005 rumors began to spread that perhaps Eminem was tired of being a rapper. These rumors suggested that he was more interested in working on the production side of music-making. However, Eminem denied the rumors.

A Real Curtain Call?

Eminem's future was uncertain. No one knew exactly where his career would go next. In 2005, some people began to say he would quit rapping.

Eminem denied the rumors. But his actions seemed to say there might be truth to them. He released an album called *Curtain Call* that year. The title suggested he was "closing the curtain," ending his career.

Would he continue making songs? Would he give it up and focus only on raising his family? Or would he find a way to be a dad and a hip-hop star?

Hip-Hop lingo

Satellite radio is a type of radio signal that is bounced off satellites and allows people to receive hundreds of different stations for a fee.
Charity is doing something to help make people's lives better.
Someone is **sober** when he is not doing drugs or alcohol.

Chapter 5

Beyond the Music

Eminem was growing into a wiser man. Things in his personal life were going much better. *Curtain Call* was a big hit. And then, just when things started to settle down, he surprised everyone by getting married again! Even more surprising—he married Kim!

A Second Chance?

The move shocked everyone. Most people thought Kim and Eminem were done for good. And the Mathers family was bigger than ever. In addition to Hailie, Alaina, and Nathan, Kim had a two-year-old daughter now named Whitney. She had given birth to Whitney while divorced from Eminem. But he decided to take care of Whitney anyway. He loved her and planned to adopt her too.

But the Mathers family never got its second chance. Eminem and Kim simply couldn't work out their differences. They divorced again after only a few months. Kim told reporters she was willing to work things out. She blamed the breakup on Eminem's ongoing drug problems. This time, their marriage was over for good.

More Trouble

A week after the divorce, Eminem took another blow. His best friend was a rapper named Deshaun Holton, also known as Proof. He was in Eminem's rap group D12. He'd been best man at his wedding. And, in 2006, he died.

Rapper Proof, actor Mekhi Phifer, and rapper Eminem perform at the *8 Mile* DVD release party in Detroit. Proof was a founding member of the rap group D12 and an influencial force in Eminem's life. He was shot and killed in April 2006.

Eminem was very sad. "He pushed me to become who I am. Without Proof's guidance and encouragement, there would have been a Marshall Mathers, but probably not an Eminem and certainly never a Slim Shady," he told reporters. "Proof and I were brothers."

Breaking the Silence

In the year after Proof's death, Eminem almost never left home. He was sad and didn't know where his life would go next. A lot of people wondered if he'd left the rap game forever. It didn't look good. He didn't release a single track in the two years after 2006. Then, one day in 2009, he released the song "Crack a Bottle." And just like that, Eminem was back.

Fans were ready for the comeback. "Crack a Bottle" broke the record for first-week download sales. It sold over 418,000 copies in its first week online. Anyone who had their doubts about Eminem's return needed to think again.

Relapse

As it turned out, "Crack a Bottle" was just the beginning. In May of 2009, Eminem released his sixth album, *Relapse*. The word "relapse" means to fall back into old ways. Eminem had relapsed into bad habits after his second divorce and Proof's death. He saw the album as a way to tell the truth about those hard years.

In the years between 2006 and 2008, Eminem struggled a lot with drugs. His depression, mixed with the drugs, made it hard to write songs. This only made him feel worse. The one thing he'd always been good at—rapping—suddenly left him! He was truly lost.

Thankfully, he chose to get help. He quit drugs and went to rehab. After he was **sober**, he found he could write lyrics again. This put him on the road to recovery.

Recovery

The word "recovery" means to get better or to return to a better self. Eminem had done just that. He'd found his voice again and started rapping once more. So *Recovery* was a good name for his next album!

Recovery sold over 700,000 copies in its first week. It was much more upbeat than any of Eminem's past albums. It gave him a chance to hope and dream for the future. Three of its songs were huge hits. "No Love," "Not Afraid," and "Love the Way You Lie" were all hit singles. After taking time off from music, there was no doubt that Eminem was back!

After *Recovery*'s success, Eminem kept making new music. In 2011, he released an album with rapper Royce da 5' 9" (part of rap group Slaughterhouse). Together, Royce and Em are Bad Meets Evil. The two rapped together on Eminem's first album. They'd been friends in Detroit before Eminem became the star we know today. But for years, they didn't talk because of a fight. After talking things over, the two decided to start hanging out again. They started working on new music together, just like they had in Detroit years ago. Soon, they had enough to put out a whole album.

The Bad Meets Evil album was a success. The album quickly sold more than 500,000 copies in the United States. The single "Lighters" (featuring singer Bruno Mars) was a huge hit.

Not Just a Musician

Eminem has other interests outside the rap game. For starters, he created Shady Records back in 2000. He spent much of his time looking for new talent. And he found it in 50 Cent, one of Shady Records' biggest stars. The superstar rapper brought lots of money to Eminem.

Eminem is still signing new rappers to Shady Records. Em signed rapper Yelawolf and group Slaughterhouse in 2011. Eminem worked on albums from both of his new acts. He was definitely back and ready to work hard to make rap fans happy.

Eminem also acted as a producer. He produced songs for 50 Cent's best-selling album *Get Rich or Die Tryin'*. He also produced

Fans reach out to touch Eminem as he performs live at the Palladium in Worcester, Massachusetts. Although rap was once a music genre confined to black ghettos, today young people of every ethnic background can connect with Eminem's sense of anger and alienation.

Eminem joins NAACP leader Dr. Benjamin Chavis, Jr., Def Jam executive Russell Simmons, Detroit mayor Kwame Kilpatrick, and rapper Nas at the 2003 Hip-Hop Summit. Dubbed "The Remix: ReBuilding, ReFocusing, ReInventing, ReSurgence," the summit offers a forum for rappers to promote positive world changes.

for The Game, Jay-Z, Lloyd Banks, Xzibit, and D12. Eminem also had the honor of producing one of Tupac Shakur's albums. After Shakur died, he left many tracks to be released. Eminem produced a Tupac album called *Loyal to the Game*.

Eminem even branched into **satellite radio** and clothing. His radio station is called Shade 45 and it's all hip-hop music. His clothing line is called Shady Ltd.

Giving Something Back

Eminem has always kept his childhood in mind. He knows that many kids grow up poor just like him. One of his goals is to help these kids live better lives. He gives some of the money from his concerts to the Boys and Girls Clubs of America. He's even won several awards in Detroit for the things he's done to help young people.

Eminem sees music as a great gift. In his own life, hip-hop gave him strength and helped him survive a difficult childhood. He supports an event in Detroit called the Hip-Hop Summit. But he's interested in more than music. He's also done concerts to make young people more aware of politics. He believes all young people should vote.

He's also done **charity** work to help fight cancer and AIDS. And he's raised money to help support fire fighters. Wherever Eminem sees a cause worth fighting for, he's there to help.

A Father's Heart

At the end of the day, Eminem is a dad. He's often said of his daughter, Hailie, "She wasn't born with a silver spoon in her mouth, but she sure has one now."

He's worked hard to help all the kids in his life—Hailie, Alaina, Nathan, and Whitney. There are a lot of unknowns in Eminem's future, but one thing is certain. He will continue to love his kids.

And he'll continue to love hip-hop too!

1972 Marshall Bruce Mathers III is born on October 17 in Saint Joseph, Missouri.

1975 Marshall's parents divorce, and Marshall never sees his father again.

1981 Marshall is badly beaten by a bully at school. He is hospitalized and suffers from recurring headaches.

1987 Marshall meets Kimberly Scott.

1995 Marshall and Kim's daughter, Hailie Jade, is born on December 25.

Marshall starts working long hours to try to support his family.

1996 Marshall begins performing under the name Eminem.

Eminem releases *Infinite*, but no one seems interested in buying his album.

Depressed by the musical failure, Eminem tries to kill himself.

1997 Eminem releases *The Slim Shady EP* and wins a hip-hop competition.

Dr. Dre signs Eminem to Aftermath Entertainment.

1999 *The Slim Shady LP* is released.

Marshall marries marries Kim Scott.

Eminem's mother, Debbie, files a $10 million lawsuit against the rapper.

2000 Eminem releases *The Marshall Mathers LP*.

Eminem is arrested twice for weapons possession and assault.

Eminem launches his own record label called Shady Records.

2001   Eminem pleads guilty to weapons charges and is put on probation. He and Kim divorce.

2002   Eminem releases *The Eminem Show*.

Eminem stars in the autobiographical movie *8 Mile*.

"Lose Yourself," a song from *8 Mile*, is nominated for an Academy Award.

2003   Eminem wins an Academy Award for his song "Lose Yourself."

2004   Eminem releases *Encore* and begins programming a hip-hop channel on Sirius Satellite Radio.

2005   Eminem cancels his European tour to enter rehab for an addiction to sleeping pills. He releases *Curtain Call*, which spurs rumors about an impending retirement.

2006   Eminem and Kim Scott remarry on January 14. Eminem files for divorce again on April 5.

2007   Eminem is on musical hiatus until 2008; he says he's been taking care of some business, and until he figures that out, he won't be releasing any new material.

2008   Though Eminem is still not touring, he lets his fans know that he is back in the studio and producing a lot of new music, thus quieting any rumors of his retirement.

2009   *Relapse* is released.

2010   *Recovery* is released after Eminem gets out of rehab for an addiction to sleeping pills.

2011   *Recovery* wins Best Rap Album at the 2011 Grammy

Awards. Eminem performs "I Need a Doctor" with Dr. Dre and Skylar Grey.

Eminem and Royce da 5'9" release a joint album as Bad Meets Evil.

Em signs rap group Slaughterhouse and rapper Yelawolf to Shady Records.

Discography
Albums

1996	Infinite
1997	The Slim Shady EP
1999	The Slim Shady LP
2000	The Marshall Mathers LP
2002	The Eminem Show
	8 Mile Soundtrack
2004	Encore
2005	Curtain Call: The Hits
2009	Relapse
2010	Recovery
2011	Hell: The Sequel (as part of Bad Meets Evil)

In Books

Baker, Soren. *The History of Rap and Hip Hop*. San Diego, Calif.: Lucent, 2006.

Comissiong, Solomon W. F. *How Jamal Discovered Hip-Hop Culture*. New York: Xlibris, 2008.

Cornish, Melanie. *The History of Hip Hop*. New York: Crabtree, 2009.

Czekaj, Jef. *Hip and Hop, Don't Stop!* New York: Hyperion, 2010.

Haskins, Jim. *One Nation Under a Groove: Rap Music and Its Roots*. New York: Jump at the Sun, 2000.

Hatch, Thomas. *A History of Hip-Hop: The Roots of Rap*. Portsmouth, N.H.: Red Bricklearning, 2005.

Websites

Dirty Dozen (his group)
www.d12world.com

Eminem
www.eminem.com

Eminem Blog
www.eminem.com/blog

MTV: Eminem
www.mtv.com/music/artist/
eminem/artist.jhtml

Shady Records
www.shadyrecords.com

Shady Records News
www.dashadyspot.com

Index

About the Author

Z.B. Hill is a an author and publicist living in Binghamton, New York. He has a special interest in adolescent education and how music can be used in the classroom.

Picture Credits